THE

UNSOLVABLE

INTRIGUE

THE
UNSOLVABLE
INTRIGUE

An Anthology of Poetry and Short Stories

D. C. Stoy

atmosphere press

*Dedicated to those who do not
give up on their dreams,
and continue to love
what is right.*

TABLE OF CONTENTS

PERSPECTIVE

HEART AND MIND

1.
Feelings have the cycle of circular reasoning,
similar to that of an ocular circumference.
Essential, yet easily agitated.

2.
Joy is like an organic fruit, a
sensation of pastel brilliance when eaten.
When never eaten, fermenting biology.

3.
Emotion is the data listings
of a mathematician. A perfectionist,
who cannot find the square root of sentiment.

4.
Feelings are not constructed in a lab, swirled
around in a translucent vile and monitored for
temperature fluctuations. They inhale without assistance.

5.
Formulas and feelings do not associate, let alone
fraternize. They observe one another in confusion
and pity; recognizing they will never integrate.

~A BLESSED MOMENT~

At this precise moment,
your lungs are swelling
with oxygen and exhaling

with carbon dioxide, vibrant and
clear. Your eyes are capturing the black
ink that appears to be *gliding* across the pale

background, with an Olympic runner's cadence.
Your nose is soaking up the satisfying scent of freshly pressed
paper, which conceals within it a recently furnished treasure chest,
    filled

to the brim with *savory*
scented perspective. Your
ears are clasping onto the barely

audible *vibrations* of your voice,
reading in hushed *whispers*, the
words that patiently lie before you.

You are blessed.

WHAT DREAMS ARE MADE OF

A distinct burnt orange leather of ambition,
interlaced with light brown threads of weaving.
The palpable American dream is another rendition,
of a hopeless night which gives the illusion of achieving.

Inner city dwellings not inhabited with wealth or gold,
forever questioning the more to life aside from blind inspiration.
Learning how to cope yet not allowing their conscience to be sold,
    using
their motivation of furthering the family legacy as a means of
    revelation.

Loose lips are not fed, but a tight-lipped shackled perspective
allows me to perhaps have a set spot in the company someday,
    thinks
the child who came from nothing, but had a keen intelligent clear
    directive.
He was taught that hard work can allow him to purchase proper
    coats...minks.

External material dreams equal to their ancestral freebooters'
visions of isolated beaches glistening with gleaming golden goblets.
We haven't changed much. Materialistic mantras are always our
    tutors,
despite what we tell ourselves. Our goals have always consisted of
    tangible objects.

Survival is the fine print on the bottom of our American Dream
Contract. We yearn for the dollar, and shun the truth for a direct
    cause:
We have families to protect, we have month-olds to feed so they
    don't scream.
Yes, survival has been in our plasma for centuries, and we did not
    inquire for applause.

The pastel thrills of aspiration and tinge of excitement that epiphany conceives is the unique innocence with which a child learns to dream *big*. What do you want to do when you grow up? But you see, how should one know their own destiny? However, these curiously carbonated concepts are what we recognize as being dreams.

And it appears that everyone has taken a swig.

I KNOW COLOR

Extensive fluidity of swaying motion and the reassuring cordiality
of a simple thought. Classiness of intrinsic mysteriousness
along with the stern solemn silent groaning of aftermath.
That was the first time I stared dead into the eyes
of the enigmatic one: *Violet.*

Fleeting dreams of a past history, a brighter day when Pharaohs
wore
the Egyptian headdresses and queens went by the names of
Nefertiti.
Epiphanies immersed in competitive tension from other nations,
resulting in historical monuments. All witnessed by the golden
piercing rays of the always observant sun. That was the
first time I held a conversation with the
knowledgeable **Canary Yellow.**

Tranquility of a majestic nature all the while being the life source
of
70% of the Earth. Embracing loyalty of raw strength reserved
through years of unparalleled experiences, producing an air
of respectability. Pure class. An introvert at heart, but can
be outgoing when called upon. A self-analyzing
paradigm with a prudent peripheral. That was
the second time I admired the brilliance of
the deservedly reserved **Teal.**

Secluded vibrance with a puddle splash of flourishing soil.
Springtime
innocence with an incomparable hearth warmth, signifying
unpolluted oxygen. Picnic authenticity of child-like
practicality. Genuinely gorgeous growth. Positively
astute and down to earth. Gracious.
There was never a time I doubted
the civility of **Forrest Green.**

I know color and color knows me.

Do you know color?

WISE CRACKS

Observationalist. I just made up a new word, and yet it makes
sense,
right? A person whose observational hobby morphs into a full-
time
occupation. Such individuals are usually regarded as having
"above-average"
intelligence, because taking time to focus on something intently, is
seen to
be a rare gift and skill, especially in today's day and **age**.

Discipline. The training of the mind to remain calm or focused in
the
midst of erratic circumstances is a lost art for us today. Few master
it, a
sliver obtain it, and the majority disregard its existence. Thinking
outside
the box is creative, but without a stable box to begin with…any
miscellaneous thought will be exalted as **brilliance**.

Reactionaries. Spur of the moment, without cognizant reasoning,
often
tends to further disturb the waters. Instantaneous decisions on
crucial matters of much needed deliberation, just adds fuel to the
already rabidly devouring fire. In truly serious matters, they
cannot be
trusted to make relatively rational **resolutions**.

Distorters. Those who reap pleasure from convoluting
imaginative yet
naïve minds. The instigators, who smear darkened diluted dye
across an
eleven-year-old's unique florescent drawing he recently created,
for kicks.
The behind-the-scenes puppeteers, who dismantle countries
and shatter inspiring dreams with a **smirk**.

The *arrogantly ignorant*. That moment, when you try to teach
a person something, but they are convinced that they have the
knowledge
and answers, so they become prideful; not knowing that they
know
absolutely nothing about the subject at all. Ultimately they have
stunted growth,
and reject learning all together. Mentors give up on them
eventually.

With all this being said, the wise take account of these normality's
and
shift through the fool's gold of plaque-infested
paradigms. Brushing away
the pride of ego, often built from entertainment misnomers can
construct a
bridge over the chasm of misunderstanding, onto the road
towards humble direction and ***intellect***.

.HOPE DOES NOT CAST A SHADOW.

Do we not all thirst for that feeling of stable certainty? The
    understanding that without a shadow of a doubt you are making the
    right choice, despite the circumstances surround
-ing your decision determined to prohibit you from clarity of thought.
    Difficulty
has often brought the best and worst out of people. True colors are
    shown
when the storm rocks the boat, causing mayhem and chaos.
Allowing a descent into the raucous waves to envelop you, blotting
out your will power to resist these overwhelming burdens, can
stifle your self-esteem. Defeat can weigh heavy on a person
who is not as confident in themselves as need be, in order
to navigate through the bedlam towards a place of up-
lifting solitude. Fighting an uphill battle can reduce
your rate of success, it might seem to the average
eye. Grasping onto the helm of the ship, and
guiding your course may appear to require
a courage you might not have. Assuming
control in a situation where all of the
odds appear to be against you, can
be a gift, a character trait. But....
we're talking reality here. And
it seems you're not there yet.
Something is holding you
back. As you stare at the
deep navy blue slapp-
ing against the sides
of the ship, you get
discouraged. This
storm is so omin-
ous. Scary I
might add.
Shadow.
You are in
need of *hope.*
Something which
does not require outside
assistance in order to aid

you in your time of need.
Hope is not something that
withholds the slashing of the
winds, restrains the raw muscle
of the menacing aquamarine depths,
nor does it completely confiscate and
conquer the storm as a whole in itself.
Hope is something which arises from the
depths of your heart. Springs up from the
recesses of your mind, to provide a foothold
upon which you place all your weight. It is
that lifejacket that always proves useful when ne-
eded. It is an inner mentality which has a unique
quality of producing an abnormal element which is
not on our periodic table. Hope comes from within, it
pivots around your mindset and develops your outlook
on life. When the storm surrounding your situations cont-
inue to rage wildly around you, it is essential that you tap
into this element. When you do, you will in turn develop clear
insight which allows you to own that calm emotional state in the
midst of the ensuing pandemonium. This might indeed sound too
good to be true, considering that your willpower alone has been push-
ed to the limit, causing your mind and body to be drained as a result of
this unfortunateness. Hope is the reinvigorated resolve that usually turns
into a self-determined leader of positive thinking. It lessens the amount
   of
negativity entering your brain when you accept the burdensome reality
   of
your stormy circumstances. It lifts those weighted dumbbells of
   opposition, and
shrouds you in a bulletproof vest of resilience, to face the storm splashing
   around you.
So, cast off the burdening cloak of fear, and embrace the glorious true
   light of hope.

((NEXT GENERATION))

Young-adult healthy interactions suffocate from societal suppression,
damaging the framework of unwarranted temptations. "Hi" just doesn't
mean "hi" anymore. Who says it? Why do they say it? Should they say it?

Kindness now readily appears as masked "advantageous" fool's gold.
Opening doors for someone has double meanings of unfathomable sensitivity.
Commenting on pleasing aroma is somehow still acceptable. For now, at least.

Independence distorted into arrogant manipulation of self-entitlement.
Kanye West's "*You can't tell me nothing*" mentality might be the best explanation.
Robust bursts of mirages illustrating a sea of uniformed asinine ambitions. *Emptiness.*

Zero unique strides or original saunters. Re-manufactured patterns
equivalent to the reemergence of past fashion creativity. *Boredom.* Or simply
just ran out of ideas. Either way, the LED screens are our new replacement pacifiers.

It is rare to notice the sunsets golden rays in another's retinas
anymore. Scare too easily now. Too timid of admiration for fear of the
social bubble being invaded. Or is it unprocessed conviction? Who knows?

Masses of vibrant fish, streaming along the current, blinded by peer
perceptions. Clones. Easily impressed with subpar entertainment,
like an infant perplexed by the game of peek-a-boo. *Wild-eyed.*

Irrational behavior justified by the notion that being young equals a pass

when it comes to entitlement. Low standards amassing statistical numbers
of record high, recycled waste idealisms. Spoon fed to young adults. *Hampering.*

Prioritization of external praise instead of inward development. Critiquing the hair
out of place instead of the inner chasm of voided morality has become the prime
concern. The constant frantic hunt for the elusive animal: *happiness,* never gets old.

But we are the future, are they not? Us young adults. With all of their
insecurities and disillusioned perceptions of what living a good life means. They
are essential to our future longevity. Can't live with us, can't live without them... *Doubtful.*

WITHDRAWALS FROM THE *FAST LANE*

Pacing is everything, in a time of sporadic decision making
made by the three and a half second intervals of devoted attention,
the people can possibly muster without straining themselves.

Pacing is crucial, in a time where the suppression of common
men's voices and thoughts are promoted as the "the right thing to
do,"
resulting in an ever-oncoming eruption of unforetold resented
emotion.

Pacing is quintessential, in a time where true jubilee has been defiled
by the onslaught of insidious divisions amongst the generations.
The relentless seeking of riches by the parents, to prove to their
predecessors that they are better at providing for their kids;
backfiring,
causing their seed to never build a potent relationship with them.

Pacing is propitious, in a time that limits the cerebral accelerations
of
artistic intellectuals, who are forced to confine their thoughts to
the bars
of desk cubicled, computational reasoning.

Pacing is fundamental, in a time where "fast lane" individuals must
deal
with the flat tires of random natural tragedy within family; which
causes
them to contemplate whether their quest for gold should be the
highest
on their totem pole.

Pacing is necessary, in a time where at the click of a button a
person's self-worth is decided by a heart or thumb emoticon

in the eyes of strangers. The fragile minds of those affected
so easily by the grandiose opinions of another,
whose blood is the same deep red as their own.

Pacing is promising, in a time where success is measured in dollars,
not
in maturity or internal stability; causing one to speak only the
language
of making money, losing the ability to understand that people's
emotions
do indeed matter.

Pacing is auspicious, in a time where life's marathon is infiltrated
with
jeers encouraging you to merge into the fast lane and race to the
finish,
without so much as one pit stop to refresh your tank, which has
been
running on low from the start.

Pace yourself, make time in your arduous schedule to focus on those
loved ones who matter, and humble your mind so it can be watered
with
a perspective of gratefulness.

The fast lane does have a finishing point, and if you get there too
soon, you'll miss out on finding true success: love for others.

WHAT DO YOU SEE?

What do you see?

I see sedimentary buildings.
Greying bricks, compound
structures aging with decades
of deteriorating tradition and
staunchly arrogant, cotton-
haired dispositions.

What do you see?

I see a respect for knowledge.
A conglomerate of visionary
geniuses discussing the future.
Yes, some are well-seasoned,
hence the fading color of their
hair follicles, however their
"staunch arrogant"
nature built our Empire.

I see sweat shops.
The anguished cries of heat-
stroke victims, derived from
steam pressed forced labor. Blank
countenances, having their ambitions
absconded by the countless hours
of systematic brainwashings.
An institutionalized hierarchical
elitism, with indentured servants.

I see a ferocious grandeur.
An unparalleled lions' strength
of will-power, battle scarred;
having suffered numerous
casualties. An admirable
feat lasting centuries,
creating a generational legacy.

Well…you're deluded.
And you're naive.
I guess we will agree to
disagree on what we see.
I guess we will.
Bring that same zeal to
your election speech.
You're going to need it.
Thank you for your concern,
same to you.
See you then.
Yeah.

[INTERIORS]

Human beings can be glass. Fragile to the touch.
Some already shattered, with just hide and creaking
skeletal structures shrouded around their stainless
dual paned innards. Remarkably transparent.

Human beings can be wood. Stout and heavy.
Weighted beams, bearing unimaginable personal
narratives. Some oak, some redwood, some ash.
Flammable to the touch. Endearing hearths.

Human beings can be stop watches. 100 meter dashers.
Plodding Clydesdales with inhibiting Velcro blinders,
driving them into fits of stampeding Thoroughbred
mania. They charge to the finish. Never once glancing back.

Human beings can be orchids. Requiring sunlight.
Meticulously sustained through solicitous warmth
and harsh frigidity. Glossy glamour spooled from
a cultivated thread of silky unrefined imperfection.

Human beings are unique.

Interiorly decorated and ornately precise.

So, human, what can you be?

HEART STRINGS

THE BLACK GLOVES

Pitch black leather gloves form-fitted to the distinct phalanges of a certain someone, whose occupation requires detailed cleaning and the intense scrubbing off of vivid vermilion vital fluid. That in itself is a chore, because most of the crimson substance is pretty much engrained in each crevasse, due to years of being rapidly smashed into the cranium of some anti-government wordsmith.

They've beheld it all, those gloves.

Witnessed the echo of muffled unorthodox whispers admonishing its owner to not fold under the pressure of looking into the eyes of these so-called "accursed free speech radicals", as they continue to spark tyrannous notions through their pen and papers. The owner, suffered a great deal with the morality of his job description, knowing in the recesses of his mind that this type of drastic censorship was *unjust*.

The black leather has sprinted through every stressed cranial hair follicle of its owner.

The smell of perfuse kerosene and the navy-blue aura of raining soot appears to be an everyday reality for the owner, after he has completed a new assignment by laying to rest not only the penmen but their dwelling place as well. The gloves abhor the flames just as much as their owner. But they love the sensation of rummaging through the ashes and skimming through the pages of notes these curious traitors have produced.

Those gloves have tasted the bitterness of anxiety when hearing:
"Just following orders",

whispered from the lips of their owner to himself, as he hauls the dead bodies of those assigned victims…*NO,* traitors, off to their malodorous trunk slung next to the others. Every time he glances at his trunk, the owner flinches, overwrought by the odor of off-white death that permeates the entire enclosure. Being a member of the secret police requires an immense amount of self-denial, a seemingly *unnatural* amount.

These black gloves have travelled to almost every region of
Europe, so they say.

One day, during an assignment in Budapest, the ebony gloves
witnessed and took part in an occurrence that they never had
before. Instead of touching the frigid hands of a corpse, they
experienced the warmth of a heavily beating quick-tempered pulse.
It appeared their owner had indeed looked into the eyes of one of
these radicals, and decided it was best to liberate them instead of
adhering to the instructions of his commanding authorities.

It was the first time those gloves felt...*shalom*?

Why he did it, even the owner did not know, but he realized that
after looking into that young woman's eyes, he noticed something
peculiar...they were strikingly *piercing*...an emerald green that
somehow surely sparked in him the humbling emotion of intense
introspection. Neither the gloves nor he could fathom why what
happened next, occurred. The owner suddenly found himself
smiling at this strange being.

It was the last time the black leather gloves tasted the metallic
acidity of gore.

The owner, cloaked in soot and hazy ashes for the first time, began
to consciously recognize the stir of his foot and the dust settling in
his heavily stressed mustache. He could not tear his gaze away from
those eyes, which somehow appeared telepathic without verbally
uttering a word. The owner started to somehow feel substances
steadily stream from of his hazel oculars, as he heard the quivering
voice of the woman.

It was the first time those gloves experienced the feeling of
degradation.

She whispered: "Are you going to kill me?" The owner and his
gloves were crying. Not sobbing. Melancholy slow tears, gently
rolling down his bristled chin hairs onto the battered black leather;
which in turn had the water droplets roll down the sides onto the
steaming sultry ground. They both hesitantly replied in unison:

"*I..don't know…*I feel strange." They did not murder the woman. They *contritely apologized* and *conversed* with her.

It was the first and last time those marred black leather gloves
and their conflicted ash-covered owner ever learned to
recognize, the priceless sacred inquisitiveness of
precious human life, and the
commendable clear skied
curiosity of…
love?

WAR'S REPETITION: THERAPY SESSION #1

Therapist: What brings you here today?

War: I keep finding myself in this patterned loop of pathetic lost-ness…I think I have entered a cycle of confusion due to my purpose being too capricious.

Therapist: Why do you think you are experiencing these feelings of "lostness" and lack of "purpose"?

War: I am lost because I find myself repeating myself over and over again recently. There was a time when I was seen to be "a last resort" due to the humans' understanding and overall respect for me. They knew what I was capable of unleashing upon them and they realized the gravity of their decisions once they let me out of my cage. My issue with struggling to find much of a purpose anymore is due to this existential crisis humanity appears to place upon me. They seriously struggle with decision making and realizing the second wave of obvious consequences come from their initial decisions.

Therapist: Overall, how would you describe your current mood?

War: I am *tired.* I am being overworked, overused, and overrun by these humans. It's like, anytime they get an excuse to put me to work, they do it. I don't know if it is just out of their pure spite for each other, or they think I am their only option when it comes to them solving problems. I truly believe that they just do not respect me anymore. They should not be infuriated with me…I am just simply doing the job they want done. Sometimes it takes six months, sometimes it takes four years. They cannot blame me for the body count that amasses; it is *their* doing.

Therapist: Why do you think that they are so swift in their reasoning to resort to your skills?

War: Exactly! I mean they know my resume'! They've seen all I have done throughout the years, the "good, the unpleasant and the atrocious"; and they know my significance. You know what I think it is...their idiotic idealisms and repetitive reasoning which blinds them to the fact that they are repeating history for just different reasons, due to this narrative they have set for themselves. And ironically when it comes back to bite them, they blame me for the blowback. I'm talking too much, aren't I? *I think I am having a mid-life crisis...who knows?*

Therapist: Has this been good for you? Venting, letting it all out...someone to talk to about this?

War: It has, it really has. Hopefully, I will get some rest for once instead of having to endure this endless loop of repetition that these lovely humans put me through for the next problem they face. Thank you again *Dr. Introspection*, I really appreciate you taking time out of your day to listen to my endless complaining.

Therapist: It is my pleasure. Stop by anytime. I'm always here to listen to you...Oh, tell your cousin, *Compromise,* to give me a call some time. I heard she needs someone to talk to as well.

War: Will do Doc'!

ADRIFT

Silently setting sail towards uncharted
territories of navy blue alluring vast expanses.
Overwhelming doubts and fears of
entering these unknown perilous regions.
Severe pressures of psychological failure analytics,
swirling around the cranium.
The course of life is a journey of uncertainty.
Of chance. A game of Blackjack.
The guidelines are never specified,
creating a hurricane of misdirection.
Navigating or letting the current guide you,
can be predicated upon self-discovery.
A scrupulous task in itself that can
last decades at a time.
For many, it takes a lifetime.
To weather the storms that arise
all the way from the Mediterranean Sea
to the Atlantic Ocean, requires
unbridled diligence. To use proactivity
as a means to construct makeshift oars,
demands ingenuity. To perceive
the blatant and subtle elemental dangers
that lurk at every wave,
necessitates cognitive self-awareness.
It can appear that you are
sailing adrift in a pool full of
quick sand. A task that is seemingly
predestined to be doomed from
its inception.

However, at your core
can lie the answer to whether or
not you will ever reach the shore.

MOTHER'S SMILE

Determined desolation of a people whose eyes are not blue and whose hair is not blonde. Whose likeness is not the same as your own, and whose religious beliefs are not directly correlated to your own. Seventy-five percent of the Jews (my people) in Europe had been annihilated. Why have we lowered ourselves to loathe one another? Are we so careless that we produce conclusions

> which cause catastrophic idealisms to corral a whole nation into angered
> fits of furnace heated rage? I can still see the smirk on your demented
> face, as you observed me gasping for air from the tears streaming down

while I witnessed my mother's last footsteps toward the showers. She smiled at me and told me to keep my head up no matter how gruesome the threats you cast at me were. That smile. It rang loud and defiantly, with the passion of warm summer in the midst of this frigid death-filled panorama of bleak hopelessness. I still have her smile.

> Your detestation does not stretch far enough to snatch that from me. I still
> live by her words, which ring loud and clear in the first pew of my mind's
> congregation as I sit in this wooden chair proudly overlooking

your trial here in the city of Nuremberg. I don't even raise an eyebrow when your lips form the sentence: "I would do it all over again if I was given the chance". As you say those words, I distinctly remember you whispering in my ear how you will break my obstinate spirit, as I heard my mother's voice start to fade away in suffocation.

> I was just a boy then, and you passed on to me the same mentally

dilapidating disease that you and your comrades inherited from the

Führer: *maniacal hatred.* In that moment, I wanted to watch you

suffocate slowly, just as my mother did. I lusted for revenge. I had to kill you. It was only right that I should. And now I am seeing it come to fruition. Here I sit, unbroken, underwhelmed, and surprisingly understanding. Hatred is something that needs no justification. It warps the mind, and now I am feeling the side effects of this disease.

Maniacal hatred is astoundingly unfulfilling. As you are sentenced to

death, I am not appeased in the slightest. Perhaps it is due to my

envisioning myself hurtling from my seat, knife in hand, aimed

for your heart, as I scream audaciously. No, I am choosing to sit still and gain satisfaction from the look in your eyes, as your conscience recognizes that your evil nature has ultimately led you to the slaughter. I will not fall victim to this disease you have implanted in me. I will not hate you. I will not take that final step towards the descent into madness on whose path you have tread all these years.

Just know that as you stroll out of this courtroom and grin at me with a

false sense of victorious accomplishment, you still suffer. I have been

healed of my hatred. I still have that memory of my mother's smile and

indomitable words. You have not broken me. My spirit has been in a reparative

state for quite some time now, while yours will be coffined under soil, eternally

digging and never grasping the contentedness of tranquility.

A HERO'S [*MASK*]

It is for your skill set that they praise you.
Your poise, resilience, and untamed
relentless refusal to be defeated,
is what grasps their attention.
Prods them to lean forward
in their padded arena seats,
salivating with anticipation.
Eager eyes, impatiently awaiting your game
determining decision. You are an athlete,
so, you must entertain. You score the
winning point, as was expected
of you. A raucous eruption
of jubilee blares from the spectators.
Yes, you too are ecstatic, but in
the press conference, your fans
cannot see that you wear a mask.
A privileged mask you might
reason. A loose muzzle of
pleasantry considering the
monetary benefits. But can you truly
be yourself? Image must be maintained.

Shuffling through the hardened steaming beige
sand with connecting shackles between
your feet. From a shadowy tunnel peering
through the slits in your helmet, you make out
the pale glow in the distance, which
is accompanied by shouts of a
ferocious nature. As you reach this
blindingly shining chorus echoing
destination, with your chains no longer
hindering your ankles, you
notice that you are carrying
a shield in one hand and brandishing
a scimitar in the other. There
are a multitude of anxious

scarlet screams surrounding you,
despite your sight being severely
limited by your cumbersome helmet.
You recognize the grotesque
nature of this call for blood. The
sickening desire to witness
two captives fight each
other to the death for survival.
You heard it during the raid
on your homeland, by invaders
from Tibullus' so-called Eternal City.
You survive the fight for your
life. Your nameless opponent
did not. As they scream
your name in psychotic glee, you close your eyes
in shame. But is that person's blood
truly on your hands? Tears
whisk down your face, mixing with the blood
soaked sand beneath your feet.
The helmet you wear, shields you. Protects
you. Masks you from this painful reality, of a
murder your hands were forced to commit.
A literal mask of self-dehumanization.
Desperately depriving you of
any form of dignity, identity, or
unique representation.

You crave the adoration.
I mean, you deserve it...do you not?
The years spent of vocal training.
The countless buckets, full of
perspiration from your time
invested in dance studios.
The competitions. You have
learned that failures are stepping stones
to success. Resilient. Resourceful. Talented.
Fashionable. You are an icon, a superstar.
And yet you wear a mask. The addictive rush of
adrenaline you receive as you come
bounding onto the stage. Oh, the

shouts of obsessive hysteria.
Your true self radiates during the course
of your performances. As you exit
however, you know it is time to don
your mask. You love your fans.
At least that's what you tell
yourself. Any decent person should
adore those who faithfully
provide your staggeringly
generous income.
And yet these benefactors
do not know you, despite their having
memorized and catalogued the history
of your vast accomplishments,
almost since your birth.
They do not see the real you, who peels
off your mask each moment you
step into your home. It gets harder
and harder to take off, doesn't it?
You must maintain an image
of insightful creativity and
relatable kinship for your
devoted fanatics. Or is it
simply toleration, as time continues to
stride forward? You have come to accept
that the cost of being
a star of superb quality is the
undeniable acknowledgment that
you will always wear the mask. The image
evolves to become more difficult
to discard, despite your determined
desire to disconnect your practiced public
persona, from the purity of your private
disposition.

Why must heroes wear masks?
Escalating to high strung
entertaining pedestals in order
to appease the masses'
neurotic yearning for

recreational satisfaction.
The talented court jesters
are still enslaved,
despite being exalted
at the same time.
They still bear the medieval
burden of dawning the mask
for us complacent never
content consumers.

COMPROMISE'S CONVERSATION: THERAPY SESSION #2

Therapist: It is a pleasure to finally meet you. Your husband, *Generosity*, has asked me to reach out to you and try to conduct at least one session.

Compromise: Oh did he now...? Hah! Always looking out for me.

Therapist: It appears that you and your husband truly have each other's best interests at heart.

Compromise: We try our best to maintain a proper balance of give and take. It's not always easy, I will tell you that.

Therapist: From your perspective, where does it appear that the problem lies?

Compromise: I wouldn't label it as a "problem". I have come to the conclusion that it is in part due to our both being positive people. I know that does not sound like anything to worry about, but I think we can be too optimistic at times without factoring in the not so positive realities of circumstantial situations.

Therapist: I see. So, what do you think is the best solution for solving this issue of only viewing the positives in these "circumstantial situations"?

Compromise: I'm no therapist or counselor, but I am pretty sure it would be wise to live in reality. Part of the issue is that he always sees the good in people. His foolish optimism blinds him to the fact that not everyone has honorable ethics and upright morality. At least that's the way it appears to me. I try to bring that balance that every substantial relationship needs, by incorporating a grounded sense of the pros and cons that can develop from our decisions. He is always trying to help someone, instead of realizing that they would not do the same for him.

Therapist: Are you saying that he is easily duped or taken advantage of, as a result of his unquenchable desire to always help his fellow man?

Compromise: You didn't happen to minor in mind reading did you, because that is exactly what I am trying to say!

Therapist: Let me ask you this: If your main skill is problem-solving and consensus establishing, and his skill is altruistic benevolence, what do you think is a proper solution?

Compromise: Well that is why I came to you *Dr. Introspection*...I was hoping you could help me figure that part out.

Therapist: Touché. Well I would advise you to sit down and speak with your husband about these issues. It is crucial that both of you speak to each other respectfully, and learn how to be attentive listeners to each other's views on the matter. In my time as a therapist and counselor, I have found that in many situations such as these, most married couples do not know how to truly listen to each other. They are just waiting for the other person to conclude their monologuing, so that they can speak.

Compromise: Yeah, we are definitely a work in progress when it comes to the listening bit. I agree. I will take some time to sit down and speak with him about this matter. I will try my best to be an active listener and hear him out. He'd better see the light soon, because I can only play the role of *Little Mrs. Sunshine* for so long...

Therapist: I am very confident that your husband will make the change you wish to see. He has your best interest at heart, considering his naturally altruistic personality. I am convinced as a result of this, your marriage will grow to be stronger for three main reasons: enhanced active listening skills, dedicated commitment to each other, and a new ability to make consensual decisions based upon weighing both the positive and negative situations.

Compromise: Well I appreciate that, Doc'. Thank you for listening to my venting. I know it must get burdensome to listen to people complain about their problems day in and day out.

Therapist: That is what I am here for. And the pleasure is all mine. I am glad that I could be a sounding board, who could lend a couple of words of wisdom. Have a great rest of your day!

Compromise: Same to you Doc'!

ANSWERS

Dear Land of the Free,

May I propose some questions to you?
What did Dr. King and Mr. X have their bodies pierced with bullets
    for?
Was it not for the freedom of an oppressed people, who have been
indoctrinated into a system of severe injustice and muffled voices?
Why has the Bald Eagle clenched the **pepper** in its talons and placed
    it in
its enclosing nest, under the guise of *"safe keeping"* from the masses
    of salt
heaps? Who decided that our **ebony** mothers must become
accustomed
to feeling abandoned and arduously burdened, with the
    responsibility
of knowing the ins and outs of your atrocious imprisonment system?
Is imprisonment and stifled freedoms what the patriots struggled
against the British to obtain, or have your history books been
    feeding
me lies? Why have you forced our desperate Robin Hoods to face
    life
sentences, all the while knowing that you have created
    circumstances
which leave that as the only option for our black fathers? Maybe
I am wrong because of my ignorance of the matter, but do you
interpret the syllables of the word freedom as the complete
domination/destruction of being free? Do you understand the
    psychological
deterioration of one's psyche after being imprisoned for ten years,
    over a
crime they know they did not commit? What must I do as a black
    young man,
to escape the cell bars which will suffocate any sign of hope for my
    future, in

this place apparently known to be the land of the free and the home
of the brave?
Please do explain, when you find some time to listen to me.

Sincerely,
D.C. Stoy

WHY DO YOU SAVE ME?

When crimson chaos catapulted
its woes in heaps upon my
calloused shoulders, and you saw
me grovel in the steaming dirt unable
to bear the weight, why did you salvage
me from the wreckage I deserved?

Countless times you have witnessed
my disgracefully meager attempts at
relying fully upon my own limited
strength; foolishly enthralled with the
theory that I can defeat such formidable
specters if I simply "believe in myself".

Oh, how wrong was I!
Completely ignorant of the fact that
without you I am floundering in the
quick sands of a barren Sahara. I am not, nor
ever will be, equipped with human weaponry
able to eradicate such immortal apparitions.

A damaged jewel is what I am.
A smeared masterpiece that falters
with every tread, continuously
stepping into potholes I have
unknowingly dug for myself. I traipse
in circles and dive into the same pitfalls.

Without you I am a repeating broken
record of stubborn arrogance. A frail-
hearted individual, lacking elasticity
of mind and spirit. Unaware of
my lack of ability to perceive my
forthcoming transgressions against you.

You continuously pardon my wrongs,
despite my endless blemished log of stubborn
actions. You comfort me in my times

of regret, and always offer me a helping hand
when I wander into peril. You liberate my confined
mind from the suffocating clutches of depression.

I have turned my back on you disrespectfully
in flurries of obstinate temper tantrumed rage,
causing you to grimace in disappointment. I hasten
back to you. My body is full of old and fresh scars.
I am apprehensive, embarrassed, and anguishing
in shame as I look upon myself. Pitiful.

Then, I see you hailing me from a distance.
Yelling my name with fervor. My eyes start
to puddle. I limp towards you, trying not to
look you in the face because of my guilt.
You sprint to my aid, and catch me before I
collapse in a mountain of exhaustion.

You weep silent tears that
speak tender words to me. Not of anger
or disappointment, but of reconciliation.
You embrace me firmly even after
my having left you. You treat my wounds, without
hesitation despite my babbling of repentance.

I know I have hurt you, time and time again.
I am not worth saving.
Yet you do so without a word.
You look upon me with affection, and replenish
Your Spirit within me. I owe you
everything, and all you ask for is for my belief.

Thank you for continuing to save me, *Adonai.*

FORGIVE MY INDISCRETION

I admit it,
I have **devoured** the
rest of the mangoes.
Summer is in its *ripeness*,
with the searing heat blaring in
through our non-tinted
windows. That sweaty severe
sensation alone drove me to
acquire the maniacal desire
to crave the golden nectar
from my most cherished
fruit in this entire universe.
I know you must have
been patiently clenching
your **molars** and biding your
time, in the hopes of consuming
this *golden delight* when it
is fully at its peak of ripeness.
I simply did not have the patience
any longer. My mouth felt as
dry as pharmaceutical cotton balls
devoid of any form of saliva.
I *had* to eat those mangoes!
I know, I was in the wrong.
I know the **anticipation** that you must
have amalgamated throughout
those days of intense yearning,
drove you almost to the point
of exhaustion. *But I simply could
not help myself!* I cannot imagine
the frustration and anger that must have
arisen on your furrowed brow when you
noticed that your **precious mangoes**
had been pilfered.

Forgive me, I know not what I do.

-NON-FORMULAIC-

Yes, two plus two are equivalent to four,
but self-guilt and anguish are not so black
and white. They are a quilted tapestry

of muted colors, dark and misty. Hazy
fog, defying the simplicity of Newton's
up and down gravitational discovery.

In that case, the apple truly does not
fall far from the tree, as seen by the
common parental anxiety that emerges

with their children who are uncertain about
their future occupation. It is a cycle, that
game of life. An emotional chess match

consisting of geometric chart-like rises
and falls. Loathing and begrudging varies
depending on what level of hatred it

amounts to on your periodic table of
bitter propensities. Only you know that.
Most do not share their truth, unless

comfortable with mediocre
feedback resulting in neither positive
or negative. They live with neutrality.

No matter the math or the science
behind it, emotional feelings of a deep
nature are unique to the individual.

So, how deep are your feelings?

No one can tell.

STORIES

-THE SCAVENGE-

Tannish brown dust-soaked desert land stretching in every course of a compasses teetering direction. Pulling up the oil stained spectacles onto patches of a rough-skinned brow, winding with

frown lines equal to those found on a 1980's city map. After spending years with a colony residing in sand dunes and hilly enclosures with the sun's blaring rays pelting down

upon you, your skin morphs into this sandpaper heap of leather. It's hard
livin' out here. Oases of lakes are a thing of the past now, and we don't even pay attention to the enticing mirages

anymore. At least we have the Nile river to guide us to the ancient ruins of
a people who have never been forgotten. But did they have to endure the scorching of the earth? Aside from the ten plagues, wars,

and Rome's ascendance there's never a time in history where the Egyptians encountered anything as brutal as the lapse in the apex (or so we like to call it). Here we trudge.

Buzzards, scavenging for the scraps left from this disarrayed burnt splintered table. A round table whose legs have been bitten to their core from years of internal termite damage

consisting of land and air pollution. Nevertheless, here we trudge, through wastelands of beige archaic feats, despite their noses being disfigured from target practice by British Soldiers.

Artifacts can be traded for the only beverage that is truly desired anymore,
yet our thirst for mere water is easily outweighed by that hope which can seemingly never be quenched…a yearning for human company.

Our small company of twenty-three people rarely comes in contact with another aimlessly wandering being, and when we do there are no words spoken. Just a hapless nod in their general direction

is their initiation into our pack. I was so excited to finally travel to
    Egypt!
Once a young historian overflowing with vigor and squirming for
adventure, without a clue about the oncoming onslaught of

insidious incineration. Fortunately, I was beneath the earth in some
ancient catacombs when I saw the flurry of singed bodies scramble
like roaches down into the depths toward me. An older man was

telling me what happened above ground, seemingly unaware that the
    left
side of his lower jaw was still smoking with sagging flesh clasped to
the dull white of his jaw bone. Blood catapulted onto me with

each word he pronounced attached to a lisp so severe, he sounded like
a teething infant trying to speak. That seemed like forever ago.
I could say that I have nightmares of the event, but I don't.

I relive it every day, but somehow it does not haunt me. Terror has
    become
my native language despite the hieroglyphics I pass by every day, for
which a younger me would have jumped for joy. Naivety,

I miss it. Now that I have witnessed the core of civilization burnt to
    death
for its foul misdeeds, my conscience yearns for the simpler times when
ignorance appeared to be frustration, but now I see it was bliss.

We scavenge to regain consciousness, not to survive. Food reawakens
    our
desire to keep existing despite our bleak landscaped circumstances.
I would desire to go West, back home to those states I thought

would forever be united. But now I ponder the possibility of more
    remorse
when those freedom monuments we Americans hold so dear are
charcoaled and crumbling amidst past flames.

I was an aspirational person at one time, now my greatest aspiration is
    to

discover whether or not we can find a sand dune to rest under tonight. Becoming a leader was definitely in the cards for me.

I just never would have guessed that I would be converted to one, under such extremely dire circumstances. So, this is where being eccentric about history gets you, I guess. In a bleak desert, with dried peeling

skin, awaiting an undesired future. Calloused as I may be, both mentally and physically; I have hope that this is a fresh slate for civilization. Maybe we can do better the second go around.

A foolish ambition, but hey, I need some sort of optimism to keep my hope
reinvigorated. I'll quit complaining now, it is tiring me out. Time to continue our scavenge and wish for a swift everlasting night.

^MY COUNTRY TIS OF THEE^

Brisk umber soil beneath my feet, seeping with years of wrongful
   raging red to
fill in the hollow gaps of all the shapes in "-gon", where glistening
   diamonds
once prevailed in what is now the streets. My grandparents would
   tell
me that there was a time when my country was known for its
majestic heritage, unparalleled natural resources,
and distinct culture.

My parents tell me South Africa is a country built on coagulated
   blood,
drugged up child soldiers, and centuries of accumulated hatred that
has compounded upon itself, due to ignorant trusting and an
infiltrated social structure. They tell me my people have
contaminated ourselves by giving in to the "white man's"
schemes, which are now even more apparent.

As I gaze out over the patiently sighing Serengeti exhaling after each
   inward
breath of tolerance, I hear my fellow adolescent friends conversing
   about
this new guy whose last name is Mandela. They tell me that he is
   the
"key to our peace to come". All I know is that since his last name
means "power", he must have something to him. We'll see if
he pans out to be our savior or a liability.

As my auditory canal captures my teacher's vibrating echo
   stretching clear
across our cringe-worthy compact classroom, I notice the slight
   quiver in
her voice as her eyes lock on a stranger in a 2B pencil-lead colored
suit. He is sitting next to my normally jovial principal who
for some strange reason is dripping sweat, stone-faced,

and has an unusually fast tapping foot.

Hope for a future away from oppression, is what I tell myself as I
    wake up to
face the day. Encouragement is the dark berry I know I must
    consume,
if I am to successfully ward off the depression that this misery
continues to cast upon me. There must be more to this life
than strife, more to life than fatigue, more to life than
survival. There must be more. And if there isn't,
then the future is pretty bleak.

TOO YOUNG TO REALIZE

I grew up mesmerized by the glorification of the American gangster,
the Edward
G's, the Cagney's, and the Bogart's. A young pup, impressed by the
big screen
and eager for the next bully to come along so I could truly see if
there was
fury in my fists. My father always told me not to seek out trouble,
and
yet I gravitated towards the *click* of the .22's trigger, as a bold
"stick-up kid". The thrill, the rush of emotion that came with
having my fellow young delinquents by my side as we ran
through the back alleys with our fists full of dollars. But
I wasn't content. I wanted more. I needed more. I still
to this day can hear my grandma admonishing me:
"He who lives by the sword, dies by the sword."
I was too young to realize... The road I was
headed down, was not merciful in the slight-
est. Years pass, more acts of violence have
my name attached to them, as I grow in
arrogance and transition from pistols
to semi-automatics. War comes,
I am eager to sign up, as are my
peers. Here I sit, in a trench,
the bodies of those once
young delinquents wrap-
ped around my feet.
Had I only realized
that my thirst for
violence led
to this. Lone
-liness...

Since its inception of teal emanating from the glistening saxophone
swaddled in the
hands of Sidney Bechet the cadence of our struggle has
emerged, plodding
intrepidly into the uncertain future without a moments
reminiscing. Moving
on is essential, is it not? To be bridled by your past history limits
your

growth, correct? But jazz is great-great grandmothers' stories of *We
Shall Overcome.*
The familiar one-two of the chain gangs' severely shackled
stride illustrated by
the snare drum's pattern of repetitive conciseness. The lightning
sharp crack of
the high-hat symbols clashing crisp and clear, equaling that of

the whistling whip eternally scarring the minds of generations to
come despite not
having witnessed it firsthand. Ebony meringue oozing from JJ
Johnson's
classic trombone, symbolizing the agonizing moans that escaped
from the
mouth of an ancestor suffering from heatstroke out in the
fields.

The sharp and heavy breaths Mammy omits when she crawls on all
fours with a giggling
four-year-old Caucasian kicking her in her sides, screaming at
her to, "*Go faster
horsy!*" Similar to that of the eager exclamations of Louis
Armstrong's raspy
trumpet, echoing defiantly in the countenances of faces so awe-
struck they grin
with an almost jeering unintentional nature. Or was it
intentional?

The dancing of the piano keys by the Duke equaling the late-night slight but anxious

pitter patting on the transparent window panes of the big house, by the blood

pricked fingers of the house slaves' less fortunate field-working brother. "*Big*

sis, please let me in…all I want is some heat!" The look of devastating real-

ization when he sees in her eyes a curious pain of uncertainty. He walks away.

Yes, the jazzy style has voiced our pain, our misfortune, and a portion of our laborious

history of oppression. And yet it eloquently details the life of our struggles with

class, crescendo, and clarity. Syncopating rhythm, emotion, and introspective

skill, allowing that conversation to occur; nurturing us through our pain in a

cadenced embrace, soothing our generations all the

while reminding us to ***never forget our past.***

(A SOLDIERS PAIN)

Clenched teeth, anguished grimaces, clouded eyes.
A quick summarization of my time out here on the
battlefield. My lungs must be filled to the brim with
virulent gasses as I sit in a barrack, amidst a platoon
of men who share a common trait. A similar uniform.

We lay in stuffy heaps, in ditches riddled with small arms
ammunition, all sincerely believing that our cause will
make the world a better place. And yet, all I can think
about is how I know this red stuff on my gloves does
not belong to me. I have witnessed so much in my life,

met so many personalities back home, made honor roll
at Notre Dame, and even enlisted with honor. It's 1941.
I have been serving my country for 3 years, and I still
cannot fathom how one man's ideology of exclusion
and eradication, can cause an entire nation to outstretch

its right arms in unison. My captain told me that's what
they do over there in Germany. I didn't believe it, at first.
I wonder what my little brother back home would say if he
saw me now. I'd be a hero in his eyes, I know I would; but
I wouldn't know how to explain to him that I never rescued

nor have even seen a single innocent person in black and
white striped pajamas. All I hear is grey commotion. All I
know is glinting barbwire. All I touch is slowing pulses.
All I taste is the bitterness of sorrow and the tang of rage.
I am not the same. How do I make this war understandable

to an 8-year-old? I myself stare at my stained uniform and
question if this is humanity's true state: the dread of knowing
our evils if stretched to the limit. How do I explain the feeling
of my numb calloused heart to a young boy, who is enthralled
with the bravado of the *American Soldier*? Big brother's college
education has been blotted out with "real world" experiences.
I'll tell him to continue his tap dancing lessons, when I get back.
If I get back. He'd be 11 now, and he will recognize that I have

become a product of the raw inhumanness of war. I need
isolation.
But I also need my family. My cause is not lost, but I am shaken.

Deeply.

How much longer must this go on?

I still can't get this blood off me!

I hate war.

I miss myself.

~I AM THE SUN~

Why must mankind always try to hide their deeds?
They think my rays will not find them. Lurking in
the shadows of their atrocious artificial homes.

I supply heat during the summer, which gives
water its true essence. I was designed to
provide hope to those who are lost. Yet you

reject me. Man thrives during my presence
and hangs me up on their walls to represent
serenity. Why do you go to darkness to believe

that true knowledge lies there? Do you not know
that I AM THE SUN! I will reveal to you what
you are looking for. Even the night cannot hold

me back, for even then I am always present.
My light will show upon the moon, giving
you that false illusion that it was she who

gives you inspiration. I was designed to
provide hope to those who are lost. Why
do you neglect me? You stay indoors and

sit on your couches when you should enjoy
my warmth and comfort. I sketch
illustrations on the horizons in the

afternoons so you do not forget me, and
yet you seem to take even this for granted.
You think your "high-tech" devices can

capture the true essence of my natural
beauty while you selfishly pose in front
of my artwork to draw attention to your

superficial smiles. I reminisce about the days
of old when man did not rely on technology

and used my light to the fullest. Why have
they forgotten me and taken me for granted?

What did I do to them? *Don't they know that I am the Sun?*

THE PHOTOGRAPH

This Black and White photograph
is clouded with grey and pale skies
which enhance two denim-jacketed
persons, who grin assumedly at an in
-side joke which lingers in the brisk
air that is shielded from their weather
-beaten faces, by the matching
dark cowboy bowl-dipping hats.

This unspoken joke which causes
them to smile in a knowing silent
chuckle speaks louder to me than
their dark Levis. Their ruffled semi-
rough collars present faces full of
memory and cattle-prodded wisdom.
Yet, I am certain that it is not cattle
they are talking about so mysteriously.

How odd is life? To know something
with a shadowed smile. Silence is the
most hilarious comedian. And know-
ledge is the elderly pall-bearer of
our experiences. They both stand
against the clouds in an assortment
of black and white. Funny how that
works. Maybe I need to be a cow-
boy to truly understand such things.

THE FOREST BEHIND LA HACIENDA
(Inspired by the Novel and Film: *The Secret Garden*)

A 10-year-old and his equally-aged friend sprint out of their
    laborious
homeschool session, in one of the archaic rooms overlooking
the forest of mystery. They had been whispering all class
period that they were going to do it! They were going
to embark into this unknown virescent sea of
Crayola colored greenery. *Oh, what an*
adventure! Father's lessons on la tradición
de la familia do not even scratch the
surface in comparison to this
thrill. They reach the forest
with giddy glee. However,
once inside, their silence
could slice through a
Redwood. The inner
woods were
gleaming
with glossy
tulips and off-white
roses. A stream jogged
throughout the center of the
enclosed terrain. Not traipsing
through, but flowing with a cadenced
finesse that added to the serenity of unique
scarlet soil that the children couldn't help but
stuff into their light blue denim pockets. Sunflower
petal-colored Parakeets swished through the lime green
thickets and singing Blue-Jays whizzed by their heads as
the kids gazed in awe at the pure beauty before them. A fawn
blinked at them, surprisingly unperturbed by their 10-year-old
presencia. It sauntered by them, unmoved in the slightest. It was
summer there, so the numerous flower colors juxtaposed in a
    satisfying
burst of whimsical joviality. Serenity at its finest. So much to
    explore! Bliss.
I wish I could go there.
To the *Forest Behind La Hacienda.*

|| SOME KINGS ARE JUST MEANT TO BE ||

Elegant Satin robes, decadent jewel-encrusted goblets, olive colognes ending in a satisfying tinge of humming mint. I have just conquered the people of Asia Minor, in its entirety, and I am only 22 years old. I will admit, observing this Persian people causes my mind to question how my father must have felt after his first victory of dominance. Was he as intrigued with the people as I clearly am?

It has taken 3 years to defeat Darius II, but somehow, I feel empty. I will go down in history as more than just the young king. *I will be* **GREAT!** Known for my ascendance to power over humanity with an Ankh in my left hand, grasping the ruby embedded handle of my lion-hilted sword, and the unbreakable golden Macedonian shield of Vergina Sun strapped to my back. But even Achilles fell.

As I unbutton the straps on my Lino thorax after a dust-filled death match, I notice a scarlet rosebud drop from a crevasse in my body armor. As the petal kisses the mat I stand upon, my mind is rushed back to my time as a young man when I am being taught by this philosopher my father assigned me. I was given this rose symbolizing that I must love myself foremost, in order to love others.

Yes, Aristotle taught me many things in my youth. As I look at these people, it is a reminder of my determined dominative destiny, but it strikes in my heart a feeling of colorless uncertainty. *I* fear no one, for *I* am that conqueror of the common world. *I* clothe my horse in golden African leopard skins, *I* adorn my breastplate with the countenance of Medusa and watch my foes turn to stone before my eyes; overwrought with trepidation. Only *I* wear the crimson-haired helmet with the bronze edifice of a true king's nature on the front: the valorous lion.

If I am honest with myself, I do not know how to be a leader of people.
I am a conqueror, not a uniter. A warrior, not a governor. A beacon.

My name is Alexander.
I will be remembered for my actions of dominance and destiny.
But…
as I look at the new faces of those I have allowed to join my
company,
I feel an emotional void.
But *I* am a king, a ruler; and *I am meant to be.*

THE INDIFFERENT DAYDREAM

The soft thistles below my feet
berate my insensitive
traipsing through their home-
stead. I casually shrug my
shoulders in juvenile
unconcern as I tug the taunt
rope that is clasped around
the leg of a Hermes-like
figure. I could tell that in
a sense, this apparition
was fully cognizant
of my innocence as a
pre-teen. My mind swiftly
shifts to a tumultuous
shadowy memory of me
noticing my unbuckled
seat belt, shards of shattered
glass racing past my pupils,
my body weight is lighter
than usual as I feel as if
I am in an amusement park
simulator ride. All I hear is
shrieking. I feel so [small] in
that space. I emerge from
that vision and take a much-
needed gulp of air
scented with pine-needles
and jasmine flowers.
I am back in the forest.
Free, light, and merry.
I feel a slight jerk
on the twine rope from
the wraith. As I glance
back I can see it violently
shaking its head as it
notices the ever-encroaching
future of where my lackadaisical
feet lead me. I stand on the

precipice of the firmament,
with my toes hanging over
the edge. The expanse
is laid bare before me in
tranquility. Could this be the
Eden that my mom would
read about to me before bed?
With a sigh, the shadow whispers
that it isn't yet my time.

But I don't want to wake up...not yet at least.

ABOUT THE AUTHOR

D.C. Stoy is an inspirational blogger (www.stoyinspiration.com), poet, and creative writer who earned his Bachelor's Degree in English from Loyola Marymount University in 2020. Coming from a basketball background, he was introduced to poetry through classes he took, which opened the floodgates for his creative writing skills to be channeled and better developed. He dedicates much of his time to honing his artistic craft through listening, learning, and especially reading. D.C. enjoys teaching and working with youth, watching films (particularly Christopher Nolan's), and has plans to pursue his Master's degree in the near future. Stoy is anticipating continuing his writing exploits as an author with more books to come. *The Unsolvable Intrigue: An Anthology of Poetry and Short Stories* is his first book.

ABOUT ATMOSPHERE PRESS

Atmosphere Press is an independent, full-service publisher for excellent books in all genres and for all audiences. Learn more about what we do at atmospherepress.com.

We encourage you to check out some of Atmosphere's latest releases, which are available at Amazon.com and via order from your local bookstore:

I Would Tell You a Secret, poetry by Hayden Dansky

Aegis of Waves, poetry by Elder Gideon

Footnotes for a New Universe, by Richard A. Jones

Streetscapes, poetry by Martin Jon Porter

Feast, poetry by Alexandra Antonopoulos

River, Run! poetry by Caitlin Jackson

Poems for the Asylum, poetry by Daniel J. Lutz

Licorice, poetry by Liz Bruno

Etching the Ghost, poetry by Cathleen Cohen

Spindrift, poetry by Laurence W. Thomas

A Glorious Poetic Rage, poetry by Elmo Shade

Numbered Like the Psalms, poetry by Catharine Phillips

Verses of Drought, poetry by Gregory Broadbent

Canine in the Promised Land, poetry by Philip J. Kowalski

PushBack, poetry by Richard L. Rose

Modern Constellations, poetry by Kendall Nichols

Whirl Away Girl, poetry by Tricia Johnson

CPSIA information can be obtained
at www.ICGtesting.com
Printed in the USA
LVHW092205300721
694164LV00004B/199